Explore **Twin Cities** OUTDOORS

HIKING

BIKING

& MORE

T0166294

Kate Havelin

MENASHA RIDGE PRESS
Your Guide to the Outdoors Since 1982

About the Author

Kate Havelin is an author, community volunteer, and outdoors enthusiast who loves exploring cities and trails. She lives in Saint Paul, Minnesota, with her husband.

Explore Twin Cities Outdoors: Your Guide to Hiking, Biking, and More

Copyright © 2018 by Kate Havelin
All rights reserved
Published by Menasha Ridge Press
Distributed by Publishers Group West
Printed in China
First edition, first printing

ISBN 978-1-63404-114-0; eISBN 978-1-63404-115-7

Design: Lora Westberg
Photos: By the author unless otherwise noted
Copy editors: Tim Jackson and Holly Cross
Proofreader: Emily Beaumont
Typesetting: Monica Ahlman
Cartography: Scott McGrew

Menasha Ridge Press
An imprint of AdventureKEEN
2204 First Ave. S., Ste. 102
Birmingham, Alabama 35233

Visit menasharidge.com for a complete listing of our books and for ordering information. Contact us at our website, at facebook.com/menasharidge, or at twitter.com/menasharidge with questions or comments. To find out more about who we are and what we're doing, visit our blog, blog.menasharidge.com.

Front cover: Minnehaha Falls via Shutterstock

Introduction

No matter where you are in the Twin Cities, parks abound. A national park runs through the Cities along the Mississippi River, whose waters shaped how Minneapolis and Saint Paul developed.

Our parks tell the tale of two cities. A century ago, a high school botany teacher helped save an undrained swamp from development. Today, that Minneapolis bog shines in the country's oldest public wildflower garden. More recently, Saint Paul citizens restored vacant brown space that the Dakota people consider sacred. What was once a railroad yard and brewery is now a nature sanctuary, opened in 2005, minutes from downtown.

Our parks and trails make this among the most livable urban areas. Minneapolis and Saint Paul have twice topped the national Trust for Public Land's Best Parks list. Minneapolis has become a city of bikes as much as lakes.

We Twin Citians like to play outdoors—biking, hiking, paddling, swimming, boating, camping, skiing, snowboarding, sledding, and snowshoeing. Park calendars are packed with archery, birding, outdoor yoga, date-night pottery sessions, stand-up paddleboarding, disc golf, geocaching, concerts, and autumn night hikes on lighted trails.

So how do you pick which park to play in? This book's 20 parks all attract hikers, and some are magnets for skiers, mountain bikers, paddlers, or swimmers. Check the indicators to the right to see which parks suit you for each season.

HIKING
BIKING
SKIING
PADDLING
SWIMMING
CAMPING

Afton State Park

AFTON STATE PARK

This spacious park on the St. Croix River spans sweeping prairies, wooded ravines, and shoreline vistas.

Difficulty: Moderate to difficult

Length/Time: 20 miles of hiking trails; 2-5+ hours, depending on pace and trail choice. Other trail types: 0.6-mile wheelchair-accessible trail ♿, 4 miles for biking, 5 miles for equestrians, 12 miles for skiing, 4 miles for snowshoeing, and 6 miles for winter walking.

Hours/Fees: Daily, 8 a.m.–10 p.m.; park office has shorter hours. State park parking permit required: $7 daily, $35 annual. Anglers need a MN fishing license. Skiers need a MN ski pass. Fees for camping and snowshoe rental. The park loans GPS units, fishing gear, birding kits, horseshoes, and volleyballs.

Getting There: *6959 Peller Ave. S., Hastings.* GPS: N44.8469°, W92.7912°

Contact: 651-436-5391, dnr.state.mn.us/state_parks/afton

Additional Information: Afton's spectacular hills and varied terrain offer a bonanza for hikers, trail runners, bikers, equestrians, and cross-country skiers. Swimmers, anglers, and campers enjoy the riverside with picnic shelters and dock, plus camping options ranging from backpack sites to cabins and yurts. Birders scope out Afton's 190-plus avian species, including eagles, turkey vultures, and 29 types of warblers.

Most trails start from the visitor center, 1.5 miles from the park office. To reach the beach, campground, and trails, you'll walk some hills. The St. Croix River sits below a 300-foot ravine, offering a cardio workout and wonderful views. Once you trek down to the river, the crushed gravel riverside trails are flat. The prairie and woodland trails roam over rolling hills and present some challenging climbs. Hill lovers should head for the steep, secluded, and splendid 5.7-mile Trout Brook Loop.

Just east of downtown Saint Paul, this hidden haven between bluffs and the Mississippi has a storied past.

Difficulty: Easy

Length/Time: About 1 mile of flat, crushed gravel hiking trail ♿ (*in summer*), plus a short loop for biking; 30 minutes–1 hour

Hours/Fees: Sunrise–11 p.m., unless otherwise posted. Although it's near downtown Saint Paul, this city park is isolated. Free.

Getting There: *265 Commercial St., Saint Paul* (parking area at Commercial and Fourth Sts.). GPS: N44.939155°, W93.046364°

Contact: St. Paul Parks: 651-266-6400, stpaul.gov/facilities/bruce-vento-nature-sanctuary; Lower Phalen Creek Project: 612-581-8636, lowerphalencreek.org

Additional Information: Named for a native East Sider and longtime congressman, this 27-acre city park opened in 2005. For centuries, the Dakota people gathered here at a sacred cave called *Wakan Tipi*, Spirit House, which is now blocked by a metal plate.

After European settlement, the cave entrance and its petroglyphs were dynamited, and marsh and forest floodplain were filled to make way for a brewery, then an industrial rail yard, and, by the 1970s, a vacant brownfield. Civic groups organized restoration efforts, which continue, and the city plans to build an interpretative center here.

Amid the new oak savanna, old concrete maintenance pads reveal glimpses of the former rail yard. National Park Service Ranger on Call signs give more history about this award-winning sanctuary. Erosion threatens the dramatic white sandstone cliff, so please stay off of it. Look and listen for songbirds, herons, grebes, hawks, and eagles, along with foxes and woodchucks, and, at times, a passing freight train.

CARVER PARK RESERVE

Wetlands and woods flourish in this park's rolling hills and restored prairie.

Difficulty: Easy to moderate

Length/Time: Nearly 26 miles of summer hiking trails, plus almost 11 miles of paved trails; 2-4 hours for the 6+ miles of turf nature center trails, depending on pace and trail choice. Other trail types: 9 miles for equestrians; 11 miles for skiing, 3+ miles for snowshoeing, and 4+ miles for winter walking.

Hours/Fees: Daily, 5 a.m.-10 p.m.; shorter hours for the nature center. Free. Fees for archery, camping, horse trails, and off-leash dog park. Ski and sled rentals available. Anglers need a MN fishing license.

Getting There: Lowry Nature Center, *7025 Victoria Drive, Victoria.* GPS: N44.882410°, W93.683322°

Contact: 763-694-7650, threeriversparks.org/location/carver-park-reserve

Additional Information: Carver's 3,700 acres include a recreation area with archery, camping (including cabins), a historic farmhouse, swimming, fishing, boating, a dog park, and the Twin Cities' first public nature center.

Opened in 1969, Lowry Nature Center features 250 acres of lakes, wetlands, and woods. It's a treat to step across the 1,700 feet of floating boardwalk over cattail marshes and swamps. Summer visitors can check out Lowry's butterfly garden and learn about prairie and rain gardens. Children can explore two distinctive play areas. In winter, Lowry's sledding hill thrills visitors, who can also strap on snowshoes or skis and hit the winter trails. Dogs are not allowed on Lowry's unpaved nature trails.

The park's varied landscapes appeal to trumpeter swans, ospreys, loons, barred owls, and some 250 species of birds, as well as muskrats, beavers, foxes, coyotes, and minks.

Tour this neat urban park with a National Park Service ranger.

Difficulty: Easy

Length/Time: Roughly 1 mile of gravel trail ♿ (*in summer*);
30 minutes–1 hour

Hours/Fees: Daily, 6 a.m.–10 p.m. Free. Coldwater's free parking fills
quickly; paid parking is nearby.

Getting There: *5601 Minnehaha Park Dr. S., Minneapolis.*
GPS: N44.901602°, W93.198256°

Contact: Mississippi River Visitor Center: 651-293-0200,
nps.gov/miss/planyourvisit/coldwater.htm

Additional Information: Wedged between Mississippi River bluffs
and Highway 55, this 29-acre Park Service site is part of the Mississippi
National River and Recreation Area. Named for the groundwater spring
that still flows year-round under an 1880s-era springhouse, Coldwater
combines history with restored prairie and oak savanna. This is consid-
ered Minnesota's first American settlement. More than a century ago,
soldiers camped here while they built nearby Fort Snelling. Then, for
a few years, Camp Coldwater was a multicultural village of settlers and
traders. More recently, Coldwater was home to the Bureau of Mines Twin
Cities Research Center. No mining happened here; instead, engineers
developed innovations in mining and space exploration.

Today, the park's spring and restored plants sustain wood ducks,
mallards, indigo buntings, eagles, turkeys, deer, and other wildlife.
From the springhouse, walk south to explore oak savanna and a ridge
trail overlooking the river valley. For longer hikes, walk south along the
paved hike/bike trail east of Coldwater to Fort Snelling or go north along
paths and sidewalks to Minnehaha Falls.

CROW-HASSAN PARK RESERVE

No other Twin Cities park can match Crow-Hassan's prairie panoramas.

Difficulty: Moderate, including some steep hills and lumpy horse trails

Length/Time: Almost 18 miles of hiking trails; the majority also allow horses and dogs; 2–3 hours for the 4.5-mile loop of mostly hiker-only trails connected by some hike/horse trails. Other trail types: 2.6 miles for skiing, 1.5 miles for snowshoeing, and 10 miles for winter walking.

Hours/Fees: Daily, 5 a.m.–10 p.m. Free. Fees for camping, skiing, horse trails, and off-leash dog areas.

Getting There: Recreation entrance/horse trailhead: *12595 Park Dr., Hanover.* GPS: N45.183170°, W93.624354°

Contact: 763-694-7860, threeriversparks.org/locations/crow-hassan-park-reserve

Additional Information: This expansive 2,600-acre park boasts more than 840 acres of restored prairie, which wows hikers, equestrians, and campers. Superb views of vibrant prairie wildflowers and the subtle sheen of tall autumn grasses distinguish Crow-Hassan.

Long pants are a good idea here, given the many insects and miles of tall grasses. In summer, there's Crow River boating and paddling and miles of walking trails. In winter, it's time for skiing, snowshoeing, dogsledding, skijoring, and walking on snow-packed trails.

The hiker-only trails start at the horse trailhead, to the left of the toilets. The turf hiking trails are easier to walk than the soft sand and lumpy gravel horse trails. The horse trails offer good views of the Crow River. Foxes, coyotes, deer, eagles, hawks, and trumpeter swans are common in this wilderness park, which shows what Minnesota looked like centuries ago.

HIKING
BIKING
SKIING
SWIMMING
CAMPING

This largest Three Rivers Park overflows with oodles of sporty options.

Difficulty: Easy to moderate

Length/Time: 51 miles of hiking trails; 2-3 hours for the 5+ miles of nature center turf trails, depending on pace and trail choice. Other trail types: 29 miles paved for biking, 14 miles for mountain biking, connections to 3 regional bike trails, 17+ miles for equestrians, 22 miles allow dogs, 19 miles for skiing, 6 miles for snowshoeing, and almost 2 miles for winter walking.

Hours/Fees: Daily, 5 a.m.–10 p.m. Free. Fees for archery, camping, disc golf, horse trails, off-leash dog area, swim pond, and many winter activities and rentals. Anglers need a MN fishing license.

Getting There: Eastman Nature Center, *13351 Elm Creek Rd., Dayton.* GPS: N45.154405°, W93.449857°

Contact: Main number: 763-694-7894, Eastman Nature Center: 763-694-7700, threeriversparks.org/location/elm-creek-park-reserve

Additional Information: This nearly 5,000-acre park boasts a wealth of trails along grasslands, restored prairies, lakes, and woods. Elm Creek's recreation includes a chlorinated swim pond, a huge play area, a historic house, archery, camper cabins, disc golf, lighted trails, snowmaking, and a 10-story-high lighted tubing hill.

The spacious new Eastman Nature Center features floor-to-ceiling windows, a screened-in deck, a quiet nature observation room, plus costumes and a puppet tree. Eastman's four loop trails—Meadowlark, Sumac, Heron/Oxbow, and Monarch—are mostly shaded and intimate. Other trails in the park are wide enough for ski teams. For a longer hike, the Monarch Trail connects to the wide Creek and Lake Trails, leading south to the swim pond, concessions, disc golf, and handsome chalet.

ELOISE BUTLER WILDFLOWER GARDEN AND BIRD SANCTUARY

Founded in 1907, this is the country's oldest public wildflower garden.

Difficulty: Easy to moderate

Length/Time: 0.6-mile trail; 30 minutes–2 hours, depending on how often you stop to snap pictures and smell the flowers

Hours/Fees: Mid-April–October 15, daily, 7:30 a.m.–1 hour before sunset, then weekends only until October 31 (visitor shelter opens at 10 a.m. Monday–Saturday and at noon Sunday). Free to enter; paid parking.

Getting There: *1 Theodore Wirth Pkwy., Minneapolis.* GPS: N44.974598°, W93.321871°

Contact: 612-370-4903, minneapolisparks.org/ebwg

Additional Information: This urban gem brims with more than 500 plant species amid charming woodlands, wetlands, and prairie. It is named for the botany teacher whose passion for wildflowers and bogs helped create this garden as Minneapolis was growing.

Chat with a naturalist at the quaint Martha Crone Visitor Shelter and maybe buy a sweetly illustrated guidebook describing the garden's 49 interpretive stations; numbered posts mark each one. Small signs identify trees and plants along the meandering trails and boardwalks.

Visit in spring, summer, and fall to gaze at the garden's progressing palette. Minnesota's rare state flower, the Showy Lady Slipper, blooms here June to early July. Especially in summer and fall, climb the hill to the prairie, alive with gaudy colors and butterflies. A water fountain and benches make it easy to stop and savor this splendid garden. Restrooms are rustic.

The Audubon Society considers this sanctuary an Important Bird Area, with 130 bird species found here. Free guided walks are offered several times weekly. No pets or trail running allowed.

FORT SNELLING STATE PARK

HIKING
BIKING
SKIING
PADDLING
SWIMMING

This park ranks among Minnesota's top 10 tourist attractions.

Difficulty: Easy (unless you climb the historic fort's strenuous hill)

Length/Time: 18 miles of summer hiking trails; 1–2 hours for the 3-mile Pike Island flat loop, depending on pace. Other trail types: 5 miles paved for biking, with connections to regional bike trails; 10 miles for mountain biking (on Dakota County side); 12 miles for skiing; snowshoeing is allowed anywhere except groomed ski trails; and 3 miles for winter walking.

Hours/Fees: Daily, 8 a.m.–10 p.m.; shorter hours for park office. Free. State park parking permit required: $7 daily, $35 annual. Skiers need a MN ski pass. Anglers need a MN fishing license, except at Snelling Lake, where MN residents can fish without a license. The park rents canoes, kayaks, and snowshoes and lends fishing gear, birding kits, and GPS units.

Getting There: *101 Snelling Lake Rd., Saint Paul* (Thomas C. Savage Visitor Center is 2 miles from the entrance). GPS: N44.891053°, W93.182537°

Contact: 612-725-2724, dnr.state.mn.us/state_parks/fort_snelling

Additional Information: At the confluence of the Mississippi and Minnesota Rivers, this park holds a central spot in state history. Dakota people lived here for centuries and consider the confluence sacred. A memorial honors the 1,600 American Indians held captive here after the U.S.-Dakota War of 1862.

On Pike Island, which the Dakota call *Wita Tanka,* Big Island, look for where the rivers meet. The Mississippi is tea-colored; the Minnesota, murky and muddy. Deer, turkeys, turtles, woodchucks, and many bird species thrive amid this Audubon Society Important Bird Area. People flock to this park to picnic, swim, boat, fish, hike, and play sports. Camping is not allowed.

9 HYLAND LAKE PARK RESERVE

HIKING
BIKING
SKIING
PADDLING
CAMPING

This big suburban park hums with four seasons of recreation on trails, slopes, and water.

Difficulty: Moderate, with some challenging hills

Length/Time: 18 miles of hiking trails, including 8+ miles of paved trails that also allow bikes and dogs; 1–2 hours for the 3+ miles of turf nature center trails, depending on pace and trail choice. Other trail types: 9+ miles for skiing, 5 miles for snowshoeing, and 1 mile for winter walking.

Hours/Fees: Daily, 5 a.m.–10 p.m. Free. Fees for boat trailer parking, camping, disc golf, snowboarding, downhill and cross-country skiing. Anglers need a MN fishing license. The park rents canoes, kayaks, rowboats, paddleboats, and winter sports gear and loans Nordic walking poles and bird-watching and bug study kits.

Getting There: Richardson Nature Center, *8737 East Bush Lake Rd., Bloomington.* GPS: N44.84301°, W93.3706°

Contact: Richardson Nature Center: 763-694-7676, threeriversparks.org /location/hyland-lake-park-reserve

Additional Information: This Three Rivers Park embraces 1,000 acres of mature woods, prairie, ponds, and a lake. A big creative play area, 27 holes of disc golf, a fishing pier, lighted trails for fall hikes and winter skiing, plus snowmaking boost Hyland's year-round appeal.

The woodchip trails around Richardson Nature Center cover a sweet mix of prairie, woods, and ponds. Look for nesting pairs of ospreys and trumpeter swans, as well as deer, foxes, turkeys, and other wildlife. For a longer hike, from the nature center trails, go south on the Osprey Trail, then continue south on grass, woodchip, or paved trails to the visitor center and scope out the snack bar, play area, water sports, and scenic Lake Trail.

HIKING
BIKING
SKIING
PADDLING
SWIMMING
CAMPING

Undulating hills of grasslands and pine forests shape this 2,100-acre park.

Difficulty: Moderate, plus some challenging hills

Length/Time: 8 miles of summer hiker-only trails, plus 14 miles of hike/ mountain bike/horse trails; 2–4 hours for the hiker-only trails, depending on pace and trail choice. Other trail types: 5 miles paved for biking ♿, 12 miles for skiing, and 2.5 miles for snowshoeing.

Hours/Fees: Daily, 6 a.m.–10 p.m. Free. Washington County parking pass required: $7 daily, $30 annual (free parking on First Tuesdays, except holidays). Fees for camping. Orienteering maps are $4. Anglers need a MN fishing license. Skiers need a MN ski pass.

Getting There: *1515 Keats Ave., Lake Elmo.* GPS: N44.970048°, W92.903167°

Contact: 651-430-8370, www.co.washington.mn.us/502/lake-elmo-park-reserve

Additional Information: This Washington County park's rolling hills beckon hikers, mountain bikers, and equestrians. The park's two large lakes, fishing pier, and chlorinated swim pond attract anglers, boaters, and swimmers. Others come for the multiple play areas, archery range, camping, and orienteering. Cross-country skiers cherish the zippy trails, of which 5.4 miles are lighted, plus lockers and changing rooms in the fine-looking Nordic Center.

The hiker-only trails, some lighted for fall hikes, are east of the park road. Start your walk at the Nordic Center trailhead. The trails pass an old red barn and border farm fields—reminders of how this land has been used. You may hear gunshots from the nearby Oakdale Gun Club. For a longer hike, take the mixed-use Eagle Point Lake loop and look for herons and other waterfowl. Pheasants, weasels, foxes, and deer also roam here.

HIKING
BIKING
SKIING
PADDLING
SWIMMING
CAMPING

Stop by the sustainably built, stylish visitor center with its plant-filled roof.

Difficulty: Moderate

Length/Time: 20 miles of summer hiking trails; 30 minutes–1 hour for the 1-mile Discovery Trail. Other trail types: 11 miles for mountain biking, 10 miles for equestrians, 19 miles for skiing, 15 miles for snowshoeing, and 1.6-mile paved trail, with 0.75-mile McDonough Lake loop. ♿

Hours/Fees: Most trailheads are open daily, 8 a.m.–10 p.m. (Holland and Jensen Lakes Trailheads open at 5 a.m.). Free. Fees for camping, horse trails, and skiing. Anglers need a MN fishing license. The park rents canoes, kayaks, stand-up paddleboards, and winter gear; loans fishing gear; and sells bait.

Getting There: Visitor center, *860 Cliff Rd., Eagan.*
GPS: N44.786483°, W93.128773°

Contact: 651-554-6530, www.co.dakota.mn.us/parks/parkstrails /lebanonhills

Additional Information: The largest Dakota County park features an array of lakes, ponds, and shelters within 2,000 acres of woods and prairie. More than half of the park's land is being or has been restored.

Lebanon has five trailheads; most hiking trails start at the visitor center trailhead by Schulze Lake or the Jensen and Holland Lakes Trailheads. (The other trailheads are primarily for mountain bikers, campers, and equestrians.) From the visitor center, walk the Discovery Trail, studded with signs about the park's landscape, wildlife, and history. For a longer hike, from the Discovery Trail, go west to the Voyageur Trail and a scenic loop around Lake Jensen, which includes a play area.

After a summer hike, go swim, paddle, and relax at Schulze Lake's beach. Don't forget to stop in the cool visitor center.

Minnehaha's fabulous waterfalls have charmed visitors for more than a century.

Difficulty: Easy (some moderate creekside trails)

Length/Time: 10 miles of mostly paved trails 🦽; 30 minutes–3 hours. Other trail types: 12.6 miles for biking, with connections to more Grand Rounds Scenic Byway trails.

Hours/Fees: Daily, 6 a.m.–midnight, developed areas (undeveloped areas close at 10 p.m.); limited hours for historic buildings and wading pool. Free entry. Paid parking (limited free parking). Fees for surrey and bike rentals, off-leash dog park, and Stevens House admission.

Getting There: *4801 Minnehaha Dr. S., Minneapolis.* GPS: N44.916121°, W93.211945°

Contact: 612-230-6400, minneapolisparks.org/parks__destinations /parks__lakes/minnehaha_regional_park

Additional Information: Opened in 1889, this immensely popular destination entertains millions of visitors, including former Presidents Lyndon B. Johnson and Barack Obama. In every season, the main attraction is the 53-foot waterfall; don't miss the wintry frozen falls. In spring, summer, and fall, hike steep stone steps to gawk at the falls gushing into Minnehaha Creek. Trails lead to a white sand beach where the creek joins the Mississippi River. The west riverside trails are more challenging.

Minnehaha's 167 acres often buzz with concerts, festivals, and charity walks. Surrey riders, walkers, runners, and bikers keep Minnehaha's paths busy. Picnickers feast at Minnehaha's large pavilion, with a restaurant and ice-cream stand, as well as the tables and shelters throughout the park, including those at Wabun Picnic Area. Wabun also has free disc golf, a wading pool, volleyball, and the city's first universally accessible play area.

HIKING
BIKING
SKIING
CAMPING

Murphy's charm is its terrain: lots of hills, few frills, and a multitude of bird species.

Difficulty: Difficult; ski maps grade these trails from least difficult to most difficult; none are easy.

Length/Time: 18+ miles of hiking, including 13 miles that also allow horses and dogs; 2–3 hours for the 3-mile hiker-only Wood Duck Trail, depending on pace. Other trail types: 10 miles for mountain biking, 9 miles for skiing, and 5.7 miles for snowshoeing.

Hours/Fees: Daily, 5 a.m.–10 p.m. Free. Fees for camping, skiing, horse trails, off-leash dog park, and boat trailer parking.

Getting There: Recreation entrance, *15501 Murphy Lake Blvd., Savage.* GPS: N44.719074°, W93.341255°

Contact: 763-694-7777, threeriversparks.org/location/murphy-hanrehan-park-reserve

Additional Information: This rustic, craggy park is a haven for hikers, mountain bikers, bird-watchers, equestrians, and skiers. At least 90 native bird species breed here, including hooded warblers, common loons, and ospreys. To protect nests at this Audubon Society Important Bird Area, some trails are closed April–August, and few allow dogs.

The main trailhead is near the park's north end, by the dog park and warming hut. Mountain bike trails start across the road. Horse trailheads are at the park's south end. The 3-mile, hiker-only Wood Duck Trail packs plenty of aerobic exercise through wavy hills past Hanrehan Lake, cattail wetlands, woods, grasslands, and boardwalk. The trail includes rocky, rooty, sandy, and sometimes muddy sections—it's a natural playground. Look and listen for the park's many woodland songbirds. For a longer hike, explore Murphy's hike-horse trails through 400 acres of restored prairie.

RTA's terrain traverses Big Woods, sedge meadow, prairie, and impressive bluff-top Minnesota River Valley panoramas.

Difficulty: Moderate to difficult

Length/Time: 5 miles of hiking trails; 2-3 hours, depending on pace and trail choice

Hours/Fees: Daily, 6 a.m.–10 p.m. Free.

Getting There: *18700 Flying Cloud Dr., Eden Prairie.* GPS: N44.818911°, W93.514413°

Contact: 952-949-8333, edenprairie.org

Additional Information: Named for an environmentalist Eden Prairie city council member, this suburban park squeezes a surprising range of terrain into 5 miles of trails. Along the way, you can read about the area's history and nature, thanks to a nonprofit group, Writers Rising Up, which crafted the many interpretive signs.

RTA includes some sharp climbs, which reward hikers with spectacular views of the Minnesota Valley National Wildlife Refuge. Atop the bluff, catch your breath as you read about the river valley's history and diverse terrains of prairie, forest, and floodplain. From the overlook, you can roam more moderate trails through a Big Woods forest of oak, maple, and hackberry trees. Posts with yellow arrows point the way through the pretty woods. You can follow the forks downhill, then wander a sedge meadow, a rare habitat of dense vegetation. Notice the masses of emerald green horsetail, also known as scouring rush, a reedy ornamental grass that thrives in soggy areas. RTA's east side includes trails through woods and prairie savanna, with a Settler's Ridge prairie savanna trailhead. The sandy exposed ridge offers a fine river valley panorama.

No bathrooms or facilities are located here.

Tour this pretty park's appealing sculptures set amid restored prairie and mature oaks.

Difficulty: Easy

Length/Time: 1+ mile of paved hike/bike/dog trails ♿, plus small sections of hiker-only turf trails; 1 hour or more, depending on pace

Hours/Fees: Daily, 5 a.m.-10 p.m.; visitor center 9 a.m.-8 p.m. (November–March, 9 a.m.–5 p.m.). Free. Fees for classes and canoe and kayak rentals. Anglers need a MN fishing license.

Getting There: *2500 County Rd. E., Saint Anthony.* GPS: N45.046809°, W93.224653°

Contact: 763-694-7707, threeriversparks.org/location/silverwood-park

Additional Information: This Three Rivers park unites art and nature, indoors and out. Silverwood's sleek visitor center showcases an art gallery with a tree ring floor design, plus a small café. All ages can see and make art at this former Salvation Army summer camp. Try yoga, photography, or date-night ceramics classes, and enjoy outdoor concerts.

Walk in any direction here to spot poetry and art installations, from the *Wetland Reclamation* sculpture on Silver Lake Island to the dramatic *High Five* sculpture overlooking the lake. Some art blends seamlessly into the environment, as with *Elevated Structure for Elevated Conversation,* a wooden pavilion by a wetland.

Near the park entrance, admire the dramatic geometric white frame, *Ylem.* Across the road, a short out-and-back dirt trail leads to a sliver of woods with picnic tables, or continue on the paved path to soak in another imaginative installation—the *S.S. Silverwood Dry Dock,* four vintage wooden boats anchored atop a grassy hill.

This Dakota County park features exceptional bluff-top vistas of the Mississippi River, which stretches more than a mile wide here.

Difficulty: Easy to moderate

Length/Time: 4+ miles of summer hiking trails, plus 6 miles of paved hike/bike/rollerblade Mississippi River Trail 🚫; 1-2+ hours for the Schaar's Bluff trails, depending on pace and trail choice. Other trail types: 5+ miles for skiing and 3 miles for snowshoeing/winter walking.

Hours/Fees: Daily, 8 a.m.-10 p.m.; Gathering Center, 8 a.m.-7 p.m. (November-March, 8 a.m.-5 p.m.). Free. Fees for archery, skiing, and community garden plot rentals.

Getting There: Schaar's Bluff Gathering Center, *8395 127th St. E., Hastings*. GPS: N44.764023°, W92.929368°

Contact: 952-891-7000, www.co.dakota.mn.us/parks/parksTrails /SpringLake

Additional Information: The multiuse paved Mississippi River Trail connects Spring Lake's two trailheads; when completed, it will span 27 miles from Saint Paul to Hastings. The West Trailhead features an archery course; the main trailhead is Schaar's Bluff, with a gorgeous Gathering Center and river panoramas. The Schaar family farmed here for almost a century before selling land in 1973 to create this park.

Check out the turf trails south and northeast of the Gathering Center; don't miss the stone bridge tucked in the woods along the northeast trail. The bridges and stone fire pit are among the fine designs that distinguish this park. As you walk through grasslands, pine forests, and woods, look for songbirds, eagles, and hawks. Pack a picnic to enjoy at tables along the phenomenal bluff, which also has a play area and sand volleyball court.

TAMARACK NATURE CENTER

This 320-acre Ramsey County preserve spans wetlands, woods, and grasslands and features a delightful play area.

Difficulty: Easy, mostly flat

Length/Time: 5.6 miles of hiking trails; 1–2 hours, depending on pace and trail choice. Other trail types: 2.5 miles for skiing, almost 2 miles for snowshoeing/winter walking, and 0.5-mile paved Bluestem Trail loop ♿.

Hours/Fees: 30 minutes before sunrise–30 minutes after sunset. Nature center: weekdays, 8 a.m.–4:30 p.m.; Saturday, 9 a.m.–5 p.m.; Sunday, noon–5 p.m. Free. Skiers need a MN ski pass. Fees for nature camps.

Getting There: *5287 Otter Lake Rd., White Bear Township.* GPS: N45.101577°, W93.038597°

Contact: 651-407-5350, tamaracknaturecenter.org

Additional Information: The fun starts before you even open the nature center's door. The Discovery Hollow Nature Play Area, next to the center's entrance, gives kids a chance to climb, crawl, garden, make dams, build tree forts, and play in mud.

Visitors of all ages can find fun on Tamarack's trails. The boardwalks—rustic, zigzagging, or new—make walking here feel like an adventure. Many of Tamarack's trails connect, so you can start on the Dragonfly Loop, passing pines and wetland along the park's north boundary, then switch to the interior Acorn Loop. Seek out the Deer Pass Trail, along the park's west and south borders, which includes lovely white birches amid aspens, maples, old oaks, and prairie. For a quick walk, try the paved Bluestem Loop and the Turtle Pass Trail. The latter leads to Tamarack Lake, a dandy spot to watch birds. No dogs or bikes allowed on Tamarack's trails.

HIKING
BIKING
SKIING
PADDLING
SWIMMING
CAMPING

Named for a lumber baron who saved white pines, this 2,200-acre park abounds with rolling meadows, marshes, prairies, forests, and some extreme slopes.

Difficulty: Easy to difficult; some roller-coaster hills

Length/Time: 16 miles of turf trails for summer hiking/winter skiing; 1.6-mile paved hike/bike/snowshoe Riverside Trail ♿; 3–4+ hours for the 5+ mile Hiking Club route, depending on pace and choice of trails.

Hours/Fees: Daily, 8 a.m.–10 p.m.; park office has shorter hours. State park parking permits are required: $7 daily, $35 annual. Skiers need a MN ski pass. Anglers need a MN fishing license. Fees for camping. The park rents canoes, kayaks, paddleboards, and snowshoes and lends GPS units, fishing gear, birding kits, horseshoes, and sports balls.

Getting There: *19074 St. Croix Trail North, Marine on St. Croix.* GPS: N45.225439°, W92.763582°

Contact: 651-433-0520, dnr.state.mn.us/state_parks/william_obrien

Additional Information: William O'Brien offers recreational options on land and water. A national Wild and Scenic River, the St. Croix attracts boaters, anglers, and paddlers. Swimmers, walkers, and snowshoers ply Lake Alice, named for the lumber baron's daughter who donated park land.

The 6-mile Hiking Club route, which starts behind the visitor center, takes you past cattail wetlands, oak-hickory forests, upland prairies, and an active railroad line. (Hikers can walk the underpass or carefully cross tracks.) The Rolling Hills Savanna and Prairie Overlook trails deliver a workout and wonderful views.

Along the trails, look for minks, foxes, raccoons, and deer. The park's many pocket gophers leave telltale clues: big dirt clumps. Nest boxes scattered throughout attract eastern bluebirds.

WOLSFELD WOODS SCIENTIFIC AND NATURAL AREA

Mature hardwoods, dainty wildflowers, and excellent birding make this rustic park a delight.

Difficulty: Easy to moderate

Length/Time: 1+ mile of hike/snowshoe trails, including some hike/horse trails; 45 minutes–1+ hours, depending on pace and trail choice

Hours/Fees: Always open; free

Getting There: Wolsfeld Woods trailhead, east side of the Trinity Lutheran Church parking lot, *2060 County Rd. 6, Long Lake*. GPS: N44.999420°, W93.574881°

Contact: DNR: 651-259-5800, dnr.state.mn.us/snas; Friends of Wolsfeld Woods: wolsfeldwoods.org

Additional Information: Thanks to maple syrup, these 220 acres are the Twin Cities' largest remaining stand of Big Woods. After settling here in 1855, the Wolsfeld family tapped, instead of cut, their maple trees.

Like all Scientific and Natural Areas, Wolsfeld is kept primitive; there are no toilets, water fountains, picnic tables, benches, or fancy bridges. Also, no dogs, bikes, or geocaching are allowed. Visitors are required to stay on trails.

Some trails are marked; others aren't. It's worth wandering these Big Woods, especially to see spring ephemerals and autumn leaves. From the trailhead sign, step into the woods and turn right to the interpretive sign. To prevent the spread of invasive garlic mustard, use the boot brush here before hiking. The trail quickly heads away from suburban backyards into the maple-basswood forest.

The DNR calls Wolsfeld a Watchable Wildlife Viewing Area, with ring-necked pheasants, Louisiana water thrushes, and nesting Acadia flycatchers. More than 150 bird species have been spotted in these lovely woods.

Known as the Marsh in the Middle of the City, Wood Lake showcases a marvelous sea of cattail marsh and floating boardwalk.

Difficulty: Easy

Length/Time: 3 miles of flat walking trails and boardwalks ⬤ *(in summer);* 1+ hours, depending on pace. Other trail types: 2+ miles for skiing.

Hours/Fees: Sunrise–11 p.m. Building open Monday–Saturday, 8:30 a.m.–5 p.m.; Sunday, noon–5 p.m. Free. Fees for classes and camps; ski, snowshoe, and community garden plot rentals.

Getting There: *6710 Lake Shore Dr., Richfield.* GPS: N44.881236°, W93.290063°

Contact: 612-861-9365, woodlakenaturecenter.org

Additional Information: Opened in 1971, Wood Lake Nature Center was the Twin Cities' first municipal nature center. The latest additions are a stone amphitheater and pollinator peace garden. This truly is an urban park, surrounded by homes and highways. Interstate 35W is just west, so you'll hear traffic here, along with the chirps and honks of redwing blackbirds, mallards, and geese.

From the interpretive center, start on the Woodland Loop, then walk the Perimeter Trail under a canopy of cottonwoods on a wide gravel path. Don't miss the Floating Boardwalk. This 0.8-mile span rewards visitors with spacious views of a big marsh; it's a terrific spot to stop and watch and listen to birds, waterfowl, and rustling reeds. Herons, egrets, woodpeckers, mergansers, chickadees, and nuthatches are among Wood Lake's many denizens.

At the park's south end, explore the Prairie Trail. Check out the nature play area by the Forest Loop; then visit the interpretive center's exhibits and animals. No pets, bikes, or rollerblades allowed.

Best For . . .

BIKERS

6 Elm Creek Park Reserve

9 Hyland Lake Park Reserve

11 Lebanon Hills
Regional Park*
(*mountain bikes)

BIRDS

7 Eloise Butler
Wildflower Garden and
Bird Sanctuary

8 Fort Snelling State Park

13 Murphy-Hanrehan
Park Reserve

HISTORY

2 Bruce Vento
Nature Sanctuary

4 Coldwater Spring

8 Fort Snelling State Park

KIDS

6 Elm Creek Park Reserve

9 Hyland Lake Park Reserve

17 Tamarack Nature Center

OFF-LEASH
DOG PARKS

3 Carver Park Reserve

6 Elm Creek Park Reserve

12 Minnehaha
Regional Park

RIVER VIEWS

1 Afton State Park

8 Fort Snelling State Park

14 Richard T. Anderson
Conservation Area

WHEELCHAIR ACCESS

12 Minnehaha Regional
Park (including playground)

15 Silverwood Park

20 Wood Lake Nature Center
(in summer)

WINTER WALKERS

4 Coldwater Spring*

8 Fort Snelling State Park*

15 Silverwood Park
(*snowshoes)

WILDFLOWERS

5 Crow-Hassan
Park Reserve

7 Eloise Butler
Wildflower Garden and
Bird Sanctuary

19 Wolsfeld Woods
Scientific and
Natural Area